# FLEECE BABIES & KIDS

LEISURE ARTS, INC • Little Rock, Arkansas

# Monster Throw

*Approximate Finished Size: 48" x 48", excluding fringe*

## SHOPPING LIST

- ☐ 1⅝ yards **each** of 2 contrasting fleeces
- ☐ masking tape

### To make the throw:

1. Cut the fleece pieces to 54" x 54" each. Stack the fleece pieces **wrong** sides together.
2. Place masking tape strips 3" in from all four sides. Cutting through both layers, cut ¾" wide x 3" deep fringe along all four sides of each fleece piece *(Fig. 1)*. Remove the tape.

Fig. 1

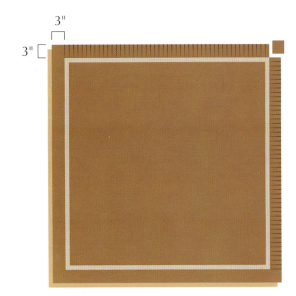

3. Using one fringe strip from each fleece piece, tie twisted knots (page 29) all the way around the throw.

# Sassy Throw

*Approximate Finished Size: 52" x 62", excluding fringe*

### SHOPPING LIST

- ☐ 1⅞ yards of fleece
- ☐ 46 yards of 6"w glittery tulle

**To make the throw:**
1. Cut the fleece to 52" x 62".
2. Make ½" long horizontal slits 1" apart along the top and bottom fleece edges, starting 1" from a side edge *(Fig. 1)*.

**Fig. 1**

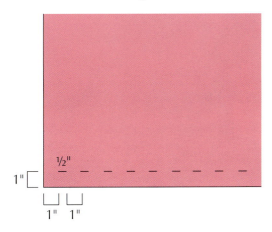

3. Cut 136 12" long strips of tulle. Holding the strips together, knot 2 tulle strips through each horizontal slit.

# Jungle Baby Throw

*Approximate Finished Size: 36" x 52"*

## SHOPPING LIST

- ☐ 1½ yards of fleece for throw
- ☐ two 36" x 7" pieces of contrasting fleece for borders
- ☐ masking tape

### To make the throw:

1. Cut the throw fleece piece to 36" x 50".
2. Matching the **wrong** sides, stack the border pieces on the the short ends of the throw piece. Place masking tape strips 3" in from the short ends. Cutting through both layers, cut ½" wide x 3" deep fringe on the ends of each fleece piece *(Fig. 1)*. Remove the tape.

**Fig. 1**

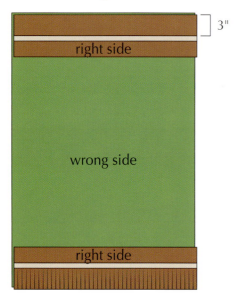

3. Using one fringe strip from each fleece piece, tie twisted knots (page 29) to join the borders to the throw.

# Jungle Baby Hat

### SHOPPING LIST
- ¼ yard fleece for hat
- motif cut from coordinating fleece, approximately 7" x 7"

**To make the hat:**
1. Measure your child's head *(Fig. 1)*:
   - around the head, just above the ears for the circumference; divide by 2 and add 1".
   - from the top of the ear to the top center of the head for the depth; add 3".

*Fig. 1*

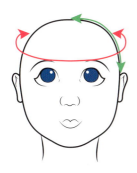

2. Cut 2 pieces of hat fleece the measurements determined in Step 1, being sure to cut the circumference measurement on the **crosswise** grain. Matching the right sides and raw edges, use a ½" seam allowance to sew the pieces together along the side and top edges *(Fig. 2)*.

*Fig. 2*

*Photo 1*

3. To hem the hat bottom, fold the fleece 1" to the wrong side and topstitch.
4. Gather the upper corners of the hat and tie with 6" x ½" fleece strips **(Photo 1)**. Securely tack the strips to the hat.
5. Stitch the motif to the hat front. We fringe-cut the lion's mane on our hat.

# Dog Hat

## SHOPPING LIST

- ☐ 1/4 yard of fleece for hat
- ☐ 1/8 yard of contrasting fleece for ears, eyes, and nose
- ☐ fleece scrap for tongue
- ☐ embroidery floss
- ☐ fabric marker
- ☐ tracing paper

*Match the right sides and raw edges and use a 1/2" seam allowance for all sewing unless otherwise noted.*

### To make the hat:

1. Trace the hat curve template and dog patterns (page 31) onto tracing paper; cut out.
2. Measure your child's head *(Fig. 1)*:
   - around the head, just above the ears for the circumference; divide by 2 and add 1".
   - from the top of the ear to the top center of the head for the depth; add 3".

**Fig. 1**

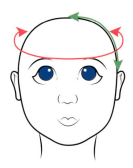

3. For the hat front and back, cut 2 pieces of hat fleece the measurements determined in Step 2, being sure to cut the circumference measurement on the **crosswise** grain; layer the pieces. Use the fabric marker to draw around the hat curve template on opposite corners of the front *(Fig. 2)*. Cut along the drawn lines through both layers.

**Fig. 2**

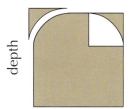

4. Use the patterns to cut 2 ears and 2 ears in reverse, 2 eyes, and a nose from the contrasting fleece. Cut a tongue from the fleece scrap.
5. Using a 1/4" seam allowance, sew an ear and a reversed ear together; clip the curves and turn right side out. Repeat to make the remaining ear.
6. Baste the ears to the hat front as shown in **Fig. 3**. Sew the hat front and back together from one lower edge, around the curved top, to the opposite lower edge. To hem, turn the lower raw edge 1/2" to the wrong side and topstitch. Turn the hat right side out.

**Fig. 3**

7. Position the eyes and nose on the hat front and use 3 strands of floss to work Blanket Stitches (page 30) around the pieces. Work a Stem Stitch mouth and French Knot cheeks. Leaving the tip free, work Running Stitches through the center of the tongue. Tack the tips of the ears to the hat front.

# Bear Hat

## SHOPPING LIST

- ☐ ¼ yard of fleece for hat and nose
- ☐ contrastrasting fleece scrap for eyes, ears, and muzzle
- ☐ embroidery floss
- ☐ fabric marker
- ☐ tracing paper

*Match the right sides and raw edges and use a ½" seam allowance for all sewing unless otherwise noted.*

### To make the hat:

1. Trace the hat curve template and bear patterns (pages 31-32) onto tracing paper; cut out.
2. Refer to Steps 2-3 of the Dog Hat, page 6, to measure your child's head and cut the hat pieces.
3. Use the patterns to cut a nose and 2 ears from the hat fleece. Cut 2 ears, 2 eyes, and a muzzle from the contrasting fleece.
4. Using a ¼" seam allowance, sew an ear and a contrasting ear together; clip the curves and turn right side out. Repeat to make the remaining ear.
5. Baste the ears to the hat front as shown in **Fig. 1**. Sew the hat front and back together from one lower edge, around the curved top, to the opposite lower edge. To hem, turn the lower raw edge ½" to the wrong side and topstitch. Turn the hat right side out.

**Fig. 1**

6. Position the eyes, muzzle, and nose on the hat front and use 3 strands of floss to work Blanket Stitches (page 30) around the pieces. Use 3 strands of floss to work a Stem Stitch mouth. Use 6 strands of floss to work French Knot pupils.

# Cat Hat

## SHOPPING LIST

- ☐ ¼ yard of fleece for hat and ears
- ☐ black fleece scrap for eyes and nose
- ☐ pink fleece scrap for ears
- ☐ embroidery floss
- ☐ fabric marker
- ☐ tracing paper

*Match the right sides and raw edges and use a ½" seam allowance for all sewing unless otherwise noted.*

### To make the hat:

1. Trace the hat curve template and cat patterns (pages 31-32) onto tracing paper; cut out.
2. Refer to Steps 2-3 of the Dog Hat, page 6, to measure your child's head and cut the hat pieces.
3. Use the patterns to cut 2 ears from the hat fleece and 2 ears from the pink fleece. Cut 2 eyes and a nose from the black fleece.
4. Using a ¼" seam allowance, sew an ear and a pink ear together; clip the curves and turn right side out. Repeat to make the remaining ear.
5. Baste the ears to the hat front as shown in **Fig. 1**. Sew the hat front and back together from one lower edge, around the curved top, to the opposite lower edge. To hem, turn the lower raw edge ½" to the wrong side and topstitch. Turn the hat right side out.

**Fig. 1**

6. Position the eyes and nose on the hat front and use 3 strands of floss to work Blanket Stitches (page 30) around the pieces. Use 6 strands of floss to work Stem Stitch whiskers.

# Dress

*Fits sizes 2T to 8.*

## SHOPPING LIST

- ☐ 1 yard of fleece for sizes 2T-5T or 1¼ yards for sizes 6-8
- ☐ two 8" pieces of ½"w elastic
- ☐ 3⅛ yards of 1½"w grosgrain ribbon
- ☐ 1⅜ yards of 1"w leopard print trim
- ☐ tracing paper

## To make the dress:

1. For the dress width, measure your child's chest across the fullest part; add 10". Make sure this is at least 5" larger than the fullest part of the hips.
2. For the dress length, measure along the child's back from the base of the neck to the desired finished length.
3. From fleece, cut a rectangle the measurements determined in Steps 1-2.
4. From ribbon and trim, cut a length the measurement determined in Step 1.
5. Sew one edge of the ribbon along the dress width 1¼" above the edge of the fleece. Overlapping the ribbon slightly, sew the trim to the fleece above the ribbon.
6. Matching the ends of the ribbon and trim, use a ½" seam allowance to sew the side seam.
7. Using the cutting line for your size, trace the arm opening template (page 32) onto tracing paper; cut out.
8. Lay the dress flat with the side seam along one side. To cut the armhole, align the straight edges of the template to the top and side seam of the dress *(Fig. 1)*; pin. Cut along the curved edge of the pattern. Repeat for the remaining armhole, aligning the template with the top and side fold.

**Fig. 1**

9. For the elastic casing, fold the top edge of the dress front 1" to the wrong side. Sew along the raw edge. Repeat for the dress back.
10. Thread the elastic through one casing. Place pins in the ends so it won't pull through as you work. Adjust the length of elastic if needed to fit the chest. Secure the elastic on each end of the casing by sewing across the ends about ¼" from the armhole edge. Repeat with the remaining casing.
11. Fold each armhole edge ½" to the wrong side; topstitch in place.
12. Cut a 10" length of trim. Aligning the trim with the casing seamline, sew the trim to the dress front, folding the ends to wrong side and trimming the ends as necessary.
13. Cut four 18" lengths of ribbon. Folding a small pleat in the end, sew a ribbon length to each end of the casings.

# Tent

## SHOPPING LIST

- 2 yards **each** of 3 contrasting fleeces
- three 72" long 1¼" dia. wood poles
- 3 rubber leg tips to fit poles
- fabric marker

### To make the tent:

1. Fold a fleece piece in half lengthwise; mark a point at the fold 64" from the bottom edge and 2½" in from the fold. Draw lines from the lower corner to the mark and from the mark to the fold *(Fig. 1)*. Cutting through both layers, cut along the drawn lines. Repeat with the remaining fleece pieces.
2. Match the right sides and raw edges and use a ½" seam allowance to sew the fleece triangles together.
3. To make each pole casing, match the wrong sides and flatten the seam area of two adjacent triangles. Topstitch 2" from the seam *(Fig. 2)*.

**Fig. 1**

**Fig. 2**

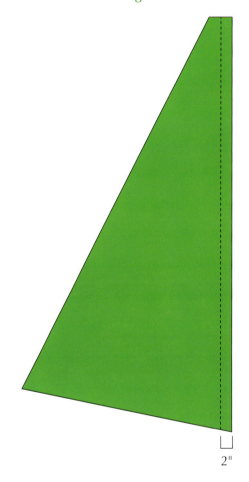

4. Insert the poles in the casings and raise the tent. Place the leg tips on the pole bottoms.
5. Cut five 1½" x 24" fleece strips. Cut a 1¼" vertical slit in the top of each triangle, 1" down from the top. Tie the poles together through the slits with 3 fleece strips.
6. Cut an opening on one side. Tie the flaps open with the remaining fleece strips by threading the strips through slits cut in the flaps and tent (on either side of the poles).

# Hooded Poncho

### SHOPPING LIST

- 2 1/8 yards of fleece for poncho and hood
- 5/8 yard of fleece for hood lining and ties
- fabric marker
- thumbtack
- string

*Match the right sides and raw edges and use a 1/2" seam allowance for all sewing unless otherwise indicated. The poncho is a complete circle with an opening for the hood cut in the middle.*

## To make the poncho:

1. Measure around your child's head just above the ears. Divide this number by 6.28 and round up to the next 1/4". This is the measurement for the neck opening. Now measure your child from wrist bone to wrist bone *(Photo 1, page 30)*, divide by 2, and add 1". This is the measurement for the length.
2. Cut a 52" fleece square. Match the right sides and fold the square in half from top to bottom and again from left to right. Tie one end of a length of string to the fabric marker; insert a thumbtack through the string at the neck opening measurement. Insert the thumbtack through the folded fleece corner. Holding the tack in place and keeping the string taut, mark the cutting line *(Fig. 1)*.

**Fig. 1**

3. Insert the thumbtack through the string at the length measurement. Insert the thumbtack through the fleece on the neck opening line; mark the cutting line *(Fig. 2)*. Cut out the poncho, cutting along both drawn lines.

**Fig. 2**

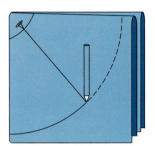

4. For the front opening, cut a 4" slit at the neck opening *(Fig. 3)*. To hem the opening, fold the cut edges 1/2" to the wrong side and topstitch.

**Fig. 3**

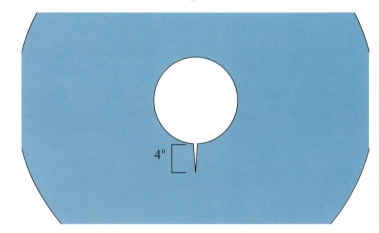

5. For the hood, measure from your child's shoulder to the top of the head; double this and add 5". Cut a fleece piece and a lining piece this measurement x half the distance around the neck opening.
6. Sew the hood and lining pieces together along one long edge.
7. Matching the seamlines, fold the sewn hood and lining in half; sew each short end together for the center back seam *(Fig. 4)*. Fold the hood over the lining and baste the bottom raw edges together. Topstitch 1/2" from the long folded edge.

**Fig. 4**

fold

center back seam

center back seam

8. Matching the openings, sew the lined hood to the poncho along the neck opening.
9. For the ties, cut two 1 1/2" x 14" strips from the lining fleece. Matching the long edges, fold each strip in half and use a 1/4" seam allowance to sew the long edges together. Turn the strips right side out. Fold one end of each strip 1/2" to one side and sew in place. Sew each remaining strip end to the neck opening.
10. Fold the poncho bottom edge 1/2" to the wrong side and topstitch in place.

# Stocking Cap

### SHOPPING LIST
- ¾ yard of fleece for cap
- ⅛ yard of fleece for pom-pom
- fabric marker

**To make the cap:**

1. Measure your child's head *(Fig. 1)*:
   - around the head, just above the ears for the circumference; divide by 2 and add 1".
   - from the top of the ear to the top center of the head for the depth; add 23".

**Fig. 1**

2. For the cap front and back, cut 2 pieces of cap fleece the measurements determined in Step 1, being sure to cut the circumference measurement on the **crosswise** grain; matching the right sides, layer the pieces. Use the fabric marker to mark the top center. Starting ½" above each lower corner, draw lines to the top center mark *(Fig. 2)*. Cut along the drawn lines through both layers.

**Fig. 2**

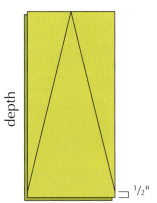

3. Matching the right sides and raw edges, use a ½" seam allowance to sew the hat pieces together along the angled edges.
4. For the bottom hem, fold 3½" to the wrong side. Topstitch 3" from the fold. Turn the hat right side out and fold the bottom up to form the cuff.
5. To make the pom-pom, cut two 4" x 15" fleece pieces. Stack the pieces. Cutting through both layers, cut ¼" wide x 1¾" deep fringe along each long edge. Roll the fringed pieces and tightly wrap the center with thread; knot the thread. Securely tack the pom-pom to the cap point.

# Beret

### SHOPPING LIST

- ☐ ⅝ yard of fleece
- ☐ fabric marker
- ☐ thumbtack
- ☐ string

*Match the right sides and raw edges and use a ½" seam allowance for all sewing. The beret is made from a crown top, crown bottom, and a band.*

## To make the beret:

1. To determine the length to cut the band, measure around your child's head over the ears and add 1". Cut a 4" wide **crosswise** fleece band the determined length.
2. Cut two 16" fleece squares. Match the right sides and fold one square in half from top to bottom and again from left to right.
3. To determine the crown bottom opening measurement, divide the band length by 6.28, subtract ½", and round up to the nearest ¼".
4. Tie one end of a length of string to the fabric marker; insert a thumbtack through the string at the determined crown bottom opening measurement. Insert the thumbtack through the folded fleece corner. Holding the tack in place and keeping the string taut, mark the crown bottom opening cutting line *(Fig. 1)*.

**Fig. 1**

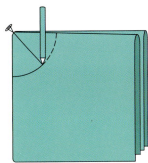

*Continued on page 18.*

# Beret continued

5. For the crown bottom outer circle measurement, add 3½" to the crown bottom opening measurement (determined in Step 3). Insert a thumbtack through the string at the outer circle measurement. Insert the thumbtack through the folded fleece corner. Holding the tack in place and keeping the string taut, mark the cutting line *(Fig. 2)*. Cut out the crown bottom, cutting along both drawn lines.

**Fig. 2**

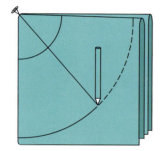

6. Use the crown bottom as a pattern to cut the crown top, cutting the **outer circle only**.
7. Sew the crown top and bottom together *(Fig. 3)*; turn right side out.

**Fig. 3**

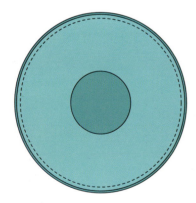

8. Sew the short ends of the band together. Fold the band in half and baste the raw edges together. Sew the band to the crown bottom opening. Fold the band to the outside.

# Pigtail Hat

## SHOPPING LIST

- ½ yard of fleece for hat
- ¼ yard of fleece for cuff
- ⅛ yard of fleece for pigtails
- fabric marker

*Match the right sides and raw edges and use a ½" seam allowance for all sewing, unless otherwise indicated.*

### To make the cap:
1. Measure your child's head *(Fig. 1)*:
   - around the head, just above the ears for the circumference; divide by 2 and add 1".
   - from the top of the ear to the top center of the head for the depth; add 3".

**Fig. 1**

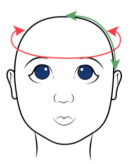

2. For the hat front and back, cut 2 pieces of hat fleece the measurements determined in Step 1, being sure to cut the circumference measurement on the **crosswise** grain. Sew the pieces together along the side and top edges *(Fig. 2)*. Turn the hat right side out.

**Fig. 2**

3. For the cuff, measure the bottom edge of the hat and add 1". Cut a 6"w fleece piece this measurement. Matching the short ends, sew the cuff piece into a ring. Matching the long edges, fold the cuff in half. Matching the right side of the cuff to the **wrong** side of the hat, sew the cuff to the hat bottom. Turn the cuff to the outside.

4. For each pigtail, cut three 1" x 19" pigtail fleece strips and a ½" x 6" hat fleece strip. Overlap the pigtail strips at one end *(Fig. 3)* and baste together. Braid the strips for about 12"; tie at the bottom with the hat fleece strip. Trim and fringe-cut the pigtail ends.

**Fig. 3**

5. Turn the hat inside out and flatten an upper corner. Insert the basted end of a pigtail into the corner from the **right** side of the hat. Stitch across the corner point, catching the pigtail end in the stitching *(Fig. 4)*. Repeat with the remaining pigtail. Turn the hat right side out.

**Fig. 4**

6. Cut two 1" x 18" cuff fleece strips for the ties. Tie a bow around each pigtail.

# Skating Skirt

## SHOPPING LIST

- 1 5/8 yards of fleece
- 1 yard of 3/4"w elastic
- 1/2 yard of 7/8"w satin ribbon
- fabric marker
- thumbtack
- string

Match the right sides and raw edges and use a 1/2" seam allowance for all sewing. The skirt is a complete circle with an elasticized waistband in the middle.

## To make the skirt:

1. To determine the measurements to draw and cut the circle, first measure your child's waist. Divide this number by 6.28 and round up to the next 1/4". This is the measurement for the waist opening. Now measure from your child's waist to the desired skirt length and add 1/2". This is the measurement for the length.
2. Cut a 52" fleece square. Match the right sides and fold the square in half from top to bottom and again from left to right. Tie one end of a length of string to the fabric marker; insert a thumbtack through the string at the waist opening measurement. Insert the thumbtack through the folded fleece corner. Holding the tack in place and keeping the string taut, mark the cutting line *(Fig. 1)*.

Fig. 1

3. Insert the thumbtack through the string at the length measurement. Insert the thumbtack through the fleece on the waist opening line; mark the cutting line *(Fig. 2)*. Cut out the skirt, cutting along both drawn lines.

Fig. 2

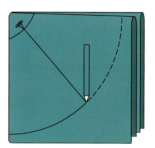

4. For the waistband, cut a 3"w fleece piece along the **crosswise** grain that is the child's waist measurement plus 1". Cut an elastic piece that is the child's waist measurement.
5. Sew the short ends of the waistband together. Overlapping the ends 1", securely sew the elastic ends together.
6. Fold the fleece waistband in half over the elastic. Baste the raw edges together.
7. Pin and sew the waistband to the skirt waist opening. Turn the waistband up. Sew a ribbon bow to the waistband front.

# Skating Hat

## SHOPPING LIST

- ³⁄₈ yard of fleece
- 1 yard of ⁷⁄₈"w satin ribbon

**To make the hat:**

1. Measure your child's head *(Fig. 1)*:
   - around the head, just above the ears for the circumference; add 1".
   - from the top of the ear to the top center of the head for the depth; add 5".

**Fig. 1**

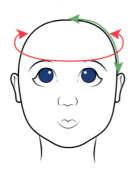

2. Cut a piece of fleece the measurements determined in Step 1, being sure to cut the circumference measurement on the **crosswise** grain. Cut 1" long vertical slits evenly spaced 1¹⁄₄" above the hat bottom edge *(Fig. 2)*. Our slits are 1" apart. Thread the ribbon through the slits. Trim the ribbon ends even with the fleece.

**Fig. 2**

circumference measurement

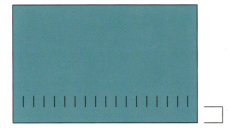

1¹⁄₄"

3. Matching the right sides and raw edges, use a ¹⁄₂" seam allowance to sew the hat together along the center back, catching the ribbon ends in the seam.
4. Cut ¹⁄₂"w x 3" deep fringe on the hat top. Gather and tie with a 15" ribbon length. Securely tack the ribbon to the hat seam.

# Skating Scarf

## SHOPPING LIST

- ¹⁄₂ yard of fleece
- 1 yard of ⁷⁄₈"w satin ribbon

**To make the scarf:**

1. Piecing as necessary, cut a 9"w fleece piece that is as long as you want the scarf, including the 3" long fringe on each end.
2. Matching the right sides and raw edges, use a ¹⁄₂" seam allowance to sew the long edges of the fleece together. Turn the scarf right side out.
3. Cut ¹⁄₂"w x 3" deep fringe on the scarf ends. Gather and tie each end with a 15" ribbon length. Securely tack the ribbons to the scarf seam.

# Tube Hat

### SHOPPING LIST

- ½ yard of fleece for hat
- ½ yard of fleece for lining
- embroidery floss

*Use 6 strands of floss for all embroidery.*

## To make the hat:

1. Measure your child's head *(Fig. 1)*:
   - around the head, just above the ears for the circumference; add 1".
   - from the top of the ear to the top center of the head for the depth; add 9".

**Fig. 1**

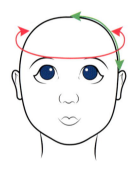

2. From **each** fleece piece, cut a piece the measurements determined in Step 1, being sure to cut the circumference measurement on the **crosswise** grain. Matching the **wrong** sides and raw edges, layer the pieces. Pin the edges together.

3. With the hat fleece facing up, fold the top edge of the layered pieces 3¼" to the hat front. Sew ¼" from the raw edge *(Fig. 2)*.

**Fig. 2**

circumference measurement

4. To fringe the top edge, make 2½" long cuts, spaced ½" apart, from the fold toward the stitching line *(Fig. 3)*. Work Blanket Stitches (page 30) across the bottom edge through both layers.

**Fig. 3**

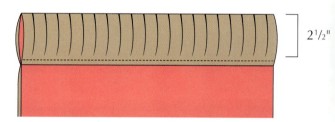

5. With the hat fleece facing up, fold up the bottom edge 3" to make the cuff. Matching the right sides and raw edges, use a ½" seam allowance to sew the hat together forming a tube; turn right side out. Gather the fringe close to the stitching line and tie securely with a 15" floss length; trim the floss ends.

# Hand Warmer Scarf

## SHOPPING LIST

- ½ yard of fleece for scarf
- ½ yard of fleece for lining
- embroidery floss

Use 6 strands of floss for all embroidery.

**To make the scarf:**

1. From each fleece, cut a 6" wide strip the desired finished scarf length plus 16", piecing as necessary.
2. Matching the wrong sides and raw edges, layer the strips. Pin the edges together.
3. With the scarf fleece facing up, fold one end of the layered strips 8" to the scarf front to form the pocket; pin. Repeat for the opposite end. Sew 3" from the fold across each end *(Fig. 1)*.

**Fig. 1**

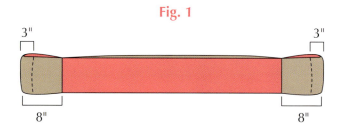

4. To fringe the ends, make 2½" long cuts, spaced ½" apart, from the fold toward the stitching lines *(Fig. 2)*.

**Fig. 2**

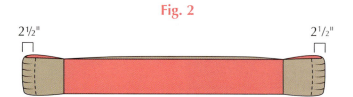

5. Stitching through the pocket layers only, work Blanket Stitches (page 30) across each pocket top. Stitching through all layers and catching the pocket sides in the stitching, work Blanket Stitches along the scarf long edges.

# Play Blocks

*Approximate Finished Size: 8" square*

### SHOPPING LIST

*For each block:*
- six 9" squares of assorted contrasting fleeces
- fabric marker
- polyester fiberfill

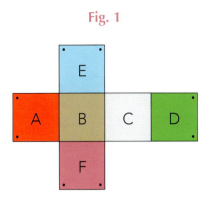

**Fig. 1**

Match the right sides and raw edges and use a $1/2$" seam allowance for all sewing.

### To make each block:

1. Mark a dot $1/2$" from each edge in the corners of each fleece square. Beginning and ending at the dots, sew the squares together *(Fig. 1)*.

2. To form the block, sew **A** and **E**, then **A** and **F** together. Sew **E** and **C**, then **F** and **C** together to make a block with an open side. Stuff the block with fiberfill. Fold the raw edges of **D** $1/2$" to the wrong side. Fold **D** over the opening and slipstitch closed.

# Leg Warmers

### SHOPPING LIST

- ½ yard of fleece
- ⅝ yard of ¾"w elastic
- 10" square of fleece for flowers
- embroidery floss
- 2 buttons
- tracing paper

**To make the leg warmers:**

1. Measure your child's leg:
   - from the knee to the ankle for the length; multiply by 1.25.
   - around the largest part of the calf; add 2".
2. Cut 2 pieces of fleece the measurements determined in Step 1, being sure to cut the calf measurement on the **crosswise** grain.
3. To make the elastic casing, fold one short end of each fleece piece 1" to the wrong side and topstitch close to the raw edge. Cut 2 elastic pieces the calf measurement determined in Step 1. Thread each elastic piece through a casing, securely stitching it at both ends *(Fig. 1)*.

**Fig. 1**

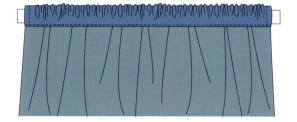

4. Matching the right sides, raw edges, and elastic ends, use a ½" seam allowance to sew each fleece piece together along the long edges, forming a tube.
5. Trace the flower patterns (page 31) onto tracing paper and cut out. Use the patterns to cut 2 large and 2 small flowers. Layer and sew a large flower, a small flower, and a button to the top of each leg warmer using 6 strands of embroidery floss.

# General Instructions

## WORKING WITH FLEECE

- Pre-washing is not necessary, however, fleece may be washed in cold water using a mild detergent on the delicate setting and tumble dried on low. Do not use bleach when washing.
- Although it is hard to see, fleece has a right side and a wrong side. Stretch the fleece on a cut edge along the crosswise grain (between the tightly woven edges); the fleece will curl to the wrong side.
- Use an all-purpose, 100% polyester thread and a size 12 (20) stretch or ball point sewing machine needle for all sewing. A longer stitch length (8-10 stitches per inch) works best. A walking foot is helpful.
- Do not press the fleece with a hot iron. Finger press when necessary.
- If you have trouble feeding the fleece through the sewing machine, loosen the pressure on the presser foot.

## TYING A TWISTED KNOT

Because this knot is twisted before you tie the second time, the contrasting fringe shows up well against the project. Stack the fleece pieces **wrong** sides together, unless otherwise indicated. Using one fringe strip from each fleece piece, tie a knot *(Fig. 1)*. Twist the fringe strips clockwise *(Fig. 2)* and tie another knot *(Fig. 3)*. Continue tying twisted knots to join the pieces.

Fig. 1

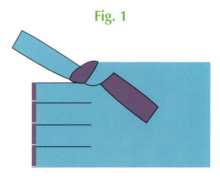

Fig. 2

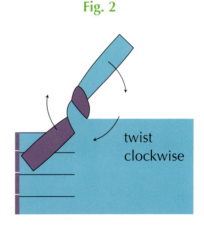

Fig. 3

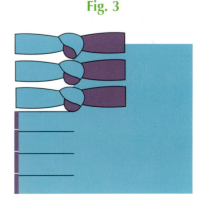

# EMBROIDERY STITCHES

When stitching, bring the threaded needle up at **1** and all **odd** numbers and down at **2** and all **even** numbers.

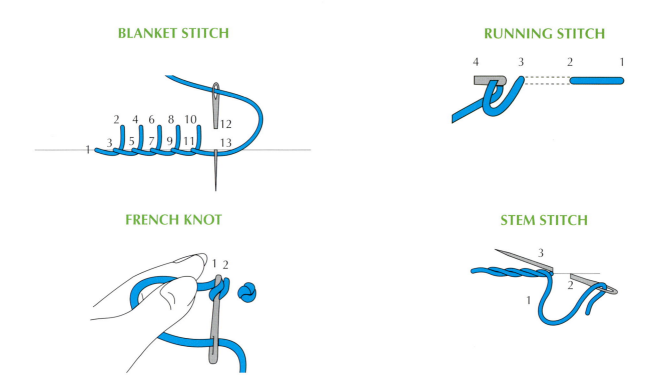

# MEASURING FOR PONCHO LENGTH

Measure your child from wrist bone to wrist bone, across her back, with her arms extended *(Photo 1)*.

**Photo 1**

# Patterns

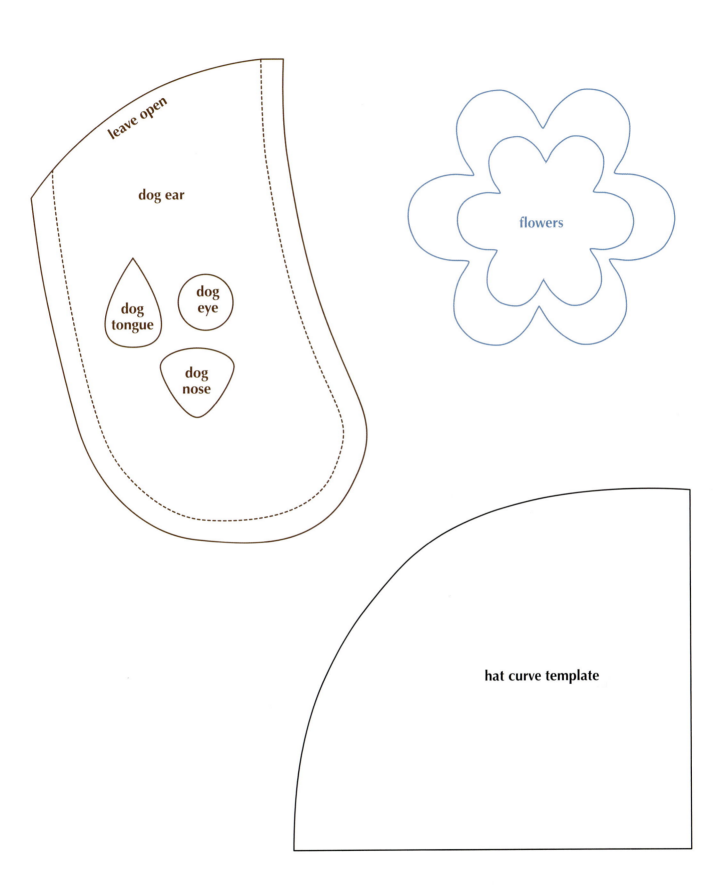

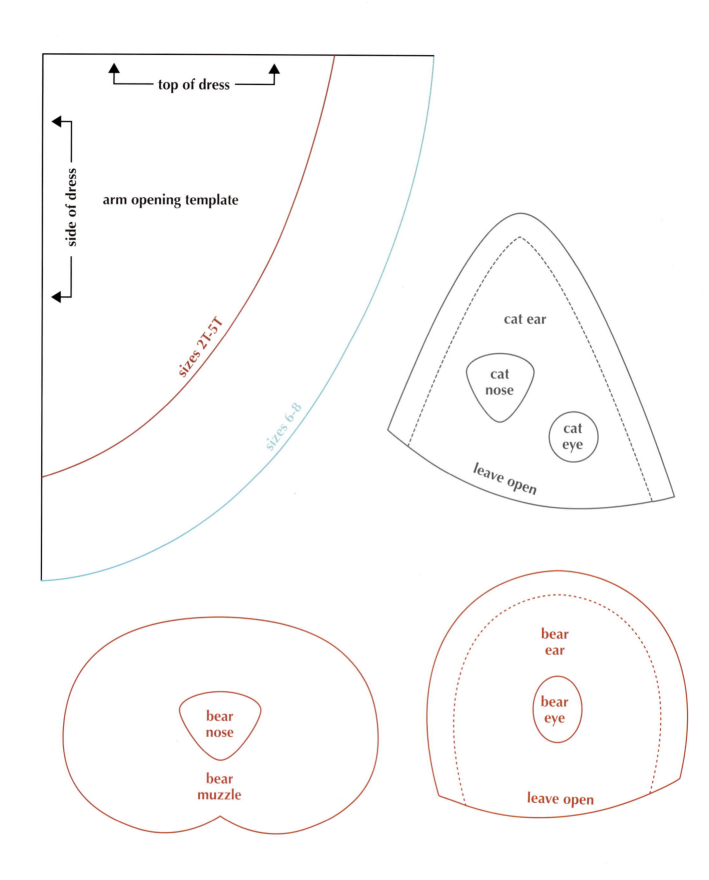